Are We Running Out of Energy?

Christiane Dorion

ARCTURUS

This edition first published by Arcturus Publishing
Distributed by Black Rabbit Books
P.O. Box 3263
Mankato
Minnesota MN 56002

Printed in the United States

Library of Congress Cataloging-in-Publication Data

Dorion, Christiane.
  Are we running out of energy? / Christiane Dorion.
      p. cm. -- (Global questions)
Includes index
ISBN 978-1-84837-013-5
1. Power resources--Juvenile literature. 2. Energy conservation--Juvenile literature. I. Title.

TJ163.23.D66 2009
333.79--dc22
                                            2008016660

9 8 7 6 5 4 3 2

Series concept: Alex Woolf
Editor and picture researcher: Patience Coster
Designer: Ian Winton
Illustrations: Stefan Chabluk

Picture credits:
Corbis: 6 (Jose Fuste Raga), 9 (Andrew K/epa), 10 (Denis Sinyakov/Reuters), 11 (Manjunath Kiran/epa),
12 (Jose Fuste Raga), 13 (Bettmann), 14 (Bettmann), 15 (Underwood & Underwood), 16 (Bettmann), 19
top (Gideon Mendel), 19 bottom (Momatiuk-Eastcott), 21 (Andreu Dalmau/epa), 23 (China
Daily/Reuters), 24 (Stuart Westmorland), 25 (Robert M. Reed/USCG/Reuters), 27 (Waltraud
Grubitzsch/dpa), 28 (Hans-Juergen Wege/epa), 30 (Bin Sheng/epa), 31 (Marcelo Sayao/epa), 34 (Car
Culture), 35 (Sergio Pitamitz), 38 (Tony West). Getty Images: 42 (Robert Nickelsberg). NASA: 22. Science
Photo Library: 17 (Philippe Psaila), 33 (Martin Bond), 37 (Martin Bond), 40 (US Department of Energy).

Cover: Oil and natural gas are burned off on an oil rig in the North Sea. The burning-off process is done to
avoid explosion or an oil slick, but it is very wasteful (George Steinmetz/Corbis).

Every attempt has been made to clear copyright. Should there be any inadvertent omission,
please apply to the publisher for rectification.

Contents

Chapter 1

Why is energy a hot issue?

To understand why energy is important, think about what you do in a single day. You wake up to the sound of an alarm clock, switch on the light, and have a hot shower. Maybe you walk to school, drive, or catch a bus. If the weather is cold, your school will be heated. When you come home, you might heat up a snack in the microwave and watch TV. All these things use energy.

Why do we need energy?

Like other living things, humans need energy to survive. We get our energy from the plants and animals we eat. It enables us to think, grow, jump, run, and dance. We have learned to harness energy from the sun to make things work for us. With energy, we make electricity and can heat or cool our homes. Energy allows cars, buses, trucks, trains, and planes to move, and with it, we can make all kinds of things, from sunglasses and sneakers to cell phones and computers.

Where does our energy come from?

Did you know that the gas in your car comes from the decay of plants and animals that lived millions of years ago, long before dinosaurs roamed the earth? Gas is derived from fossil fuels, which took a long time to form.

The Bund, shown here lit up at night, is one of the most famous streets in Shanghai, China. As the world's cities grow and energy demands increase, the way we produce, distribute, and use energy is damaging the environment.

Oil and gas were created from the remains of tiny marine animals buried at the bottom of the ocean. Long after the prehistoric seas vanished, these animal remains were compressed by heat and pressure. Oil was formed first, but in deeper and hotter areas, the "cooking" process continued until natural gas was formed. The same process also created coal from the remains of trees and ferns.

Why do we need to change our energy use?

Today fossil fuels provide 85 percent of our energy. Until recently, they were the cheapest source of energy. Oil powers 90 percent of the world's transportation, and coal is the most popular fuel for generating electricity. Natural gas is used mainly for heating. But there are two huge problems with using fossil fuels. First, they are nonrenewable because they take millions of years to form and can only be used once. If we keep using them as we are now, nearly all of the existing reserves will be gone by the end of the twenty-first century. Second, when we burn fossil fuels, we produce polluting gases that contribute to warming the earth's temperature. This is why we need to find alternatives.

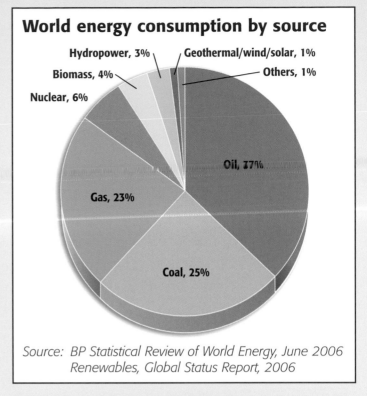

World energy consumption by source

Hydropower, 3%
Geothermal/wind/solar, 1%
Biomass, 4%
Others, 1%
Nuclear, 6%
Oil, 37%
Gas, 23%
Coal, 25%

Source: *BP Statistical Review of World Energy, June 2006 Renewables, Global Status Report, 2006*

Most of our energy comes from oil, coal, and natural gas, which will run out someday. Only 8 percent of our energy comes from renewable resources.

FOCUS

And then there was light...

Lhaba, a 33-year-old farmer, used to light her stone house in the remote village of Zem in Tibet with candles and lights made from butter oil. In June 2006, a new solar power plant started to supply her house and the homes of 44 other families. Lhaba now has electric lights, a television, and a machine to make butter tea. With 3,000 hours of sun per year, Tibet has the highest potential for solar power in the world, after the Sahara desert. Access to energy will help improve the villagers' standards of living.

Going nuclear

Some countries rely partly on nuclear power, another nonrenewable source of energy. Nuclear power is generated through nuclear fission, a process that involves splitting tiny particles called atoms. Every object in the universe is made up of atoms. By splitting the bonds that hold atoms together, an enormous amount of heat can be released. This energy can be harnessed to generate electricity. Currently, about 6 percent of the world's energy comes from nuclear power. The fuel most widely used for this process is uranium, which is extracted from the earth. Many people are against nuclear power because its production creates highly toxic waste that takes more than 20,000 years to decay.

Using renewables

Only 8 percent of our energy comes from renewables; in other words, sources that can be replaced. Day after day, the sun shines, the wind blows, water flows, and trees grow. These are all potential sources of energy. Many of them have been used on a small scale for hundreds of years. We have learned to design buildings that capture the heat of the sun, and over the centuries, we have used the power of the wind to mill flour and transport goods and people. Wood is still used in many countries for heating and cooking. But the use of renewable energy on a large scale costs more than burning fossil fuels, which means that so far, it has not been a favored option.

In places such as China, Canada, Brazil, and the United States, hydropower is an important source of renewable energy. These countries have high mountains and fast-flowing rivers, so they have the right geography for harnessing the power of falling and moving water. To generate hydropower, a river is dammed to form a reservoir. The dam regulates the flow of water. A large area needs to be flooded to create a reservoir, and villages are sometimes relocated in the process.

Expert View

Many experts agree that energy supplies are limited, so we must look for alternative sources of energy in the future:

"There is about 40 years' worth of oil reserves at the current production rates. For gas, we know of 70 years' worth of reserves. For coal, there is at least 160 years, with estimates up to 1,000 years because no one has gone seriously exploring for coal."

Iain Conn, director of British Petroleum, speaking in 2006

The Three Gorges Dam on the Yangtze River in China is the world's largest hydroelectric power station. More than 1 million people had to be relocated so that the reservoir could be built.

Who owns the energy resources?

Ownership of energy resources depends mostly on luck. Reserves of fossil fuels are spread unevenly around the world. One-quarter of the world's coal reserves are found in the United States, while more than half the world's oil is in the Middle East. The main reserves of uranium for nuclear power are in Australia, Canada, and Kazakhstan. If a country has plentiful resources, it is in a strong position because it can produce goods, run a transportation system, and supply the energy people need.

Arguments over energy

Some countries have so much coal, oil, gas, or uranium that they sell it to other countries. Others have very few reserves and need to import their energy. The quest for energy resources can become a source of conflict. For example, many people believe the world's dependence on Mideastern oil has increased the potential for wars in that area. Discovering new reserves can also cause problems. As the earth's temperature has risen with our burning of fossil fuels, the Northwest Passage, a sea route through Northern Canada, has opened up. Until recently, this route, which connects Europe and Asia, was often frozen solid. But the ice at the North Pole has melted so much that the waterways are now

A worker welds part of a pipeline that will carry natural gas from Siberia in Russia to Western Europe. The project should be completed by 2010.

FORUM

People hold very different views about who should have access to the world's energy supplies:

"Energy is essential for development. Yet 2 billion people currently go without, condemning them to remain in the poverty trap. We need to make clean energy supplies accessible and affordable."

Kofi Annan, United Nations secretary-general (1997–2007), speaking in 2002

"We will not do anything that harms our economy, because first things first are the people who live in America; that's my priority."

President George W. Bush, 2001

What's your view?

more navigable. Many countries are rushing to claim the possible reserves of oil and other minerals there and are beginning to lay claim to the area.

How is energy used around the world?

Different countries use different amounts of energy. The United States has only 5 percent of the world's population, but its citizens consume 26 percent of the world's energy. Per person, Canada consumes the most energy in the world. Not everyone depends on fossil fuels. More than a century after the invention of the lightbulb, nearly one-third of the world's population still does not have electricity. Most of these people live in rural areas in South Asia and Africa. Their main sources of energy for cooking, lighting, and heating are wood and animal waste. They need access to other types of cheap energy to improve their standards of living.

A woman returns from collecting firewood in a village on the south coast of India. Many people around the world still rely on wood for cooking and heating their homes.

Why does energy hit the news?

Energy issues make news headlines for a variety of reasons. The world's population is increasing rapidly, as is its demand for energy. Countries such as China, Brazil, and India have fast-growing economies. Just a few years ago, traffic jams were unheard of in the Chinese capital city, Beijing. In China today, one family in four owns a car. Two hundred years ago, everyone would have relied on the fuel they could find around their homes. Today the energy for our fuel, heat, and light travels long distances to reach us. Finally, the way we produce, distribute, and use energy is harmful to the environment. Stories about the environment make news, whether they are about the waste created by extracting coal or spills of uranium or oil caused by transporting fuel around the world. But the most serious threat affecting everyone in the world is the fact that the earth is being heated to dangerous levels by our burning of fossil fuels. Humans are contributing to a major change in the earth's climate.

Chapter 2

What is the story of energy?

Early humans learned to make fire by rubbing pieces of flint together. This was the beginning of an incredible journey of discovery and invention that harnessed energy resources to meet people's needs. Until 150 years ago, most of the energy we used came from renewable sources such as the sun, wind, trees, and flowing water.

The first sources of energy

About 5,000 years ago, Egyptians made the first known sailing boats, capturing the wind to travel faster and farther. About 2,500 years ago, the Persians used the wind to power windmills to crush grain. At the same time, the Greeks were building homes to take advantage of the sun's light and warmth. They were also piping water from hot springs to heat their houses. By the end of the Roman era, waterwheels were providing power in mills to crush grain, shape iron, and saw wood.

Ancient civilizations also discovered they could use fossil fuels for lighting and heating. Egyptians learned to collect oil floating on the surface of lakes and use it as fuel or medicine. The ancient Chinese learned to pump natural gas from shallow wells; they

Feluccas (sailing boats) on the Nile River in Egypt. For about 5,000 years, people have used the wind as a source of energy to move people and goods around the world.

This engraving from 1835 shows workers at a textile factory during the Industrial Revolution. The mass production of textiles in factories meant an increasing demand for energy.

used the gas to heat seawater and extract salt from it. They also discovered they could burn coal and produce heat. During the Middle Ages, people throughout Europe channeled moving water to turn wooden wheels to grind grain. Engineers built mills on boats and bridges, and industrial areas sprang up along rivers. In the sixteenth and seventeenth centuries, European explorers used the power of the wind to propel their sailing ships across oceans to discover new lands.

FOCUS

Working in a coal mine

In 1842, 10-year-old Alexander Gray was working as a pump boy in a coal mine. He described his daily life: "I pump out the water in the under-bottom of the pit to keep the men dry. I am obliged to pump fast or the water would cover me. The water frequently covers my legs. I have been two years at the pump. I am paid 10 old pence a day. No holiday but the Sabbath [Sunday]. I go down at three, sometimes five in the morning, and come up at six or seven at night."

The age of machines

The world changed significantly during the eighteenth and nineteenth centuries, when the Industrial Revolution started in England. Textiles, pottery, iron, and steel had traditionally been produced in small workshops, but the Industrial Revolution meant that they began to be made in factories. This mass production by machine meant the demand for energy increased rapidly. Many of Europe's forests were cut down to fuel the production of iron and the building of ships. Coal was the most popular fuel, but it was hard to extract because the mines were constantly filling up with groundwater.

Full steam ahead

In 1705, Thomas Newcomen invented the steam engine. This technological wonder was developed by James Watt and provided the solution to flooded coal mines. When attached to a pump, it enabled miners to pump the water out of the mines and dig deeper in their search for coal. Steam power quickly spread to factories and to transportation. The steam locomotive was developed in 1804, the steamboat in 1807, and in 1825, the first steam railway opened. The new methods of transport allowed raw materials and goods to be moved more quickly and cheaply than ever before. As industry forged ahead, the production of cheaper sources of energy and the popularity of fossil fuels increased.

Electricity takes over from steam: in 1938, a steam locomotive pulls into a railroad station in Philadelphia. A new electric locomotive stands ready to leave on its first official run.

Light in the darkness

About 130 years ago, electricity was produced mainly through hydropower, near fast-flowing rivers. In 1882, Thomas Edison founded the first power station on Pearl Street in New York to produce and distribute electricity. Edison's distribution system sent electricity to 85 buildings, powering 5,000 lights. This invention would change the industrial world dramatically in the twentieth century. It meant that machines powered by electric motors could be used anywhere, far away from rivers and steam power plants. Street railways drawn by horses or powered by steam quickly became a thing of the past as electric streetcars took over. Electricity replaced gas and kerosene for lighting and wood and coal for cooking. There was a drawback, however: to produce electricity, another source of energy was needed. So the demand for energy increased again.

Oil

In 1859, a former train conductor named Colonel Edwin Drake made an extraordinary discovery. He drilled down and extracted crude oil out of the ground at his well in Titusville, Pennsylvania. By using a steam engine to power the drill, Drake managed to pump the oil up to the surface. Studies of crude oil revealed that many useful products, such as kerosene and gasoline, could be made from it. With the hugely popular development of the automobile in the early 1900s, gasoline gradually became the most important fuel of the twentieth century. However, in 1973 panic spread across America and Europe. Some oil-rich Mideastern countries cut off their exports to

the West because they were angry about its involvement in a conflict that was taking place between Israel and several Arab countries. As a result, oil companies increased their prices massively. In the 1990s, Iraq's invasion of Kuwait, a country rich in oil, also resulted in an increase in oil prices. These events prompted many governments to look for different sources of energy.

Edwin Drake conceived the idea of drilling oil out of the ground in Titusville, Pennsylvania, in 1859. Here he stands (wearing a top hat) next to his original oil rig.

> ## Expert View
>
> **For a variety of reasons, inventors and entrepreneurs have long been interested in developing alternative sources of energy:**
>
> "The fuel of the future is going to come from fruit like that sumach [tree] out by the road, or from apples, weeds, sawdust—almost anything. There is fuel in every bit of vegetable matter that can be fermented. There's enough alcohol in an acre of potatoes to drive the machinery necessary to cultivate the field for a hundred years."
>
> *Henry Ford, inventor and founder of the Ford Motor Company, quoted in the* **New York Times, 1925**

Splitting the atom

In 1905, scientist Albert Einstein discovered that matter and energy could not be created or destroyed; they could only be changed in form. This amazing finding, along with the work of physicist Marie Curie in the nineteenth century on the structure of uranium atoms, led to the discovery of nuclear power.

In the late 1930s, as the world entered World War II, physicists in Europe and the United States came to understand that splitting a uranium atom could release enormous amounts of energy. In 1942, they conducted tests that produced nuclear energy. Their work led to the production of the atomic bomb. By 1957, the first commercial nuclear power plant was in operation, and nuclear plants were built around the world to meet the increasing demand for energy.

In 1905, scientist Albert Einstein found that matter and energy could not be created or destroyed; they could only be changed in form. This led to the discovery of nuclear power.

However, nuclear power was not without its problems. In 1979, a major accident occurred at the Three Mile Island nuclear power plant in Pennsylvania. Another disaster took place in 1986 at the Chernobyl nuclear power plant in Ukraine, where a reactor exploded and sent a radiation plume (cloud) across Europe. As a result, many countries, including Italy and Germany, stopped relying on nuclear power. The argument against this new form of energy was also strengthened by the safety hazards involved in the disposal of radioactive waste.

Early environmentalists?

Until relatively recently, people always relied on renewable sources of energy. At the time of the Industrial Revolution, forward-thinking scientists were researching ways to capture the power of the sun, the wind, flowing water, and the earth's internal heat to generate energy. For example, in 1860, Auguste Mouchout, a French mathematics teacher, was so concerned that coal reserves in Europe would one day be depleted that

FORUM

In the past, some scientists believed a future energy crisis would change the way the world works. But some businesspeople today still do not think there is an energy crisis:

"Eventually industry will no longer find in Europe the resources to satisfy its prodigious expansion. Coal will undoubtedly be used up. What will industry do then?"

Auguste Mouchout, inventor, 1860

"We're doing great. The American economy is flourishing. We're using more fossil fuels. We're putting more CO_2 in the air. The coal plants are running at record levels. Business has never been better."

Fred Palmer, Western Fuels Association, 2000

Do you agree with either of these opinions?

he developed the first motor to run on solar power. In 1900, thousands of tidal mills dotted the coasts of North America and Europe. In the same year, Rudolph Diesel used peanut oil to fuel the first bio-diesel engine. But these great inventions were often ignored and delayed because cheaper sources of energy were readily available.

With the depletion of fossil fuels and the increasing pollution of the earth, we might have to return to renewable sources. Today scientists are trying to develop these technologies to make them more efficient, affordable, and reliable. In the end, perhaps our over-reliance on fossil fuels will feature as just a short blip in the history of humanity.

Workers build a steam generator for a nuclear power plant in France. There are more than 440 nuclear power stations in the world today, providing about 8 per cent of the world's energy.

Chapter 3

Why is the climate changing?

For nearly 200 years, people have been changing the earth's atmosphere by burning coal, oil and gas on a large scale and pumping out massive amounts of carbon dioxide and other gases. Many scientists now believe that these human activities are one of the major causes of climate change.

Is the earth really warming up?

In 1988, the United Nations set up the Intergovernmental Panel on Climate Change, which employed hundreds of top scientists to look into the issue of global warming. The scientists concluded that global warming really is occurring, and they are 90 percent certain that the cause is human activity. The earth's temperature is warming faster than at any time in the past 10,000 years. This has a huge impact on the climate.

As the oceans warm up, there is more water vapor in the air, which means more rainfall. But this rainfall is not evenly distributed throughout the world. While some areas have experienced more heavy rain and floods, other areas, for example, southern Australia and parts of Africa, have suffered more heat waves and droughts. Extreme weather events, such as hurricanes and tropical storms, have become more frequent. The poles are warming up twice as fast as the rest of the world, and Greenland's ice sheet is

FOCUS

Climate change refugees

The 980 inhabitants of the Carteret Islands in Papua New Guinea have become the first climate change refugees. For more than 30 years, they have battled against the Pacific Ocean to stop the waves crashing over their homes. They have struggled to protect their fruit trees and coconut palms from destruction by salt water. But every year, the tidal surges have become stronger and more frequent, and in 2005, the people were evacuated to a larger island nearby. By 2015, their islands are likely to be completely submerged beneath the Pacific.

A man stands outside his house in the Indian village of Pir-muhammadpur on the banks of the Ganda River. The area was submerged by flooding in August 2007.

slowly disappearing. The Arctic has lost about a third of its ice since satellite measurements began 30 years ago. Snow is receding from the mountains of Canada, China, Peru, Africa and Europe. This has an impact on rivers and on our water resources.

Rising sea levels

As the oceans gradually became warmer during the twentieth century, ice melted and sea levels rose by about 8 inches (20 cm). This doesn't sound like much, but it has already had an impact on people living on islands in the Pacific and on coasts of low-lying countries such as Bangladesh. Global warming is also affecting wildlife because habitats are changing. Polar bears face the loss of their icy wilderness in the Arctic, and they are forced to swim farther in their hunt for seals. The penguin population in Antarctica has declined in the last 25 years because the krill they eat is becoming scarce. Spring arrives earlier now, and this means that mosquitoes, birds, and other creatures that like warm weather are broadening their territories. Many species of fish are moving north to cooler waters, and the migration routes of some birds, fish, and turtles are changing.

South Georgia Island in the South Atlantic Ocean is the most important penguin nesting and breeding area on earth. But the ice is melting fast because of global warming, and the penguin population is in decline.

The greenhouse effect

Our earth and its atmosphere are like a greenhouse. Sunlight energy enters the atmosphere. As it reaches the earth's surface, some of this energy is absorbed by the land, the water, and the trees, and some is reflected back into the atmosphere. But much of the heat remains, trapped by natural "greenhouse" gases, which include carbon dioxide, methane and nitrous oxide. This natural "greenhouse effect" causes the world to stay warm. Without it, heat would escape back into space and life on earth would not be possible: it would be far too cold.

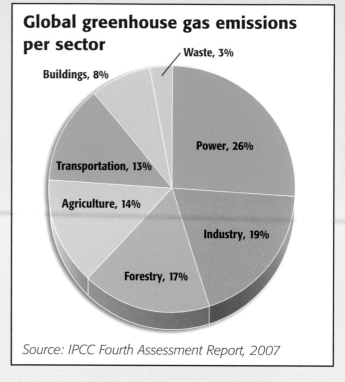

Global greenhouse gas emissions per sector

- Waste, 3%
- Buildings, 8%
- Power, 26%
- Transportation, 13%
- Agriculture, 14%
- Industry, 19%
- Forestry, 17%

Source: IPCC Fourth Assessment Report, 2007

Human activity has resulted in the concentrations of greenhouse gases being higher now than at any time during the last 650,000 years. There is about 30 percent more carbon dioxide and double the amount of methane in the atmosphere today as there was before the Industrial Revolution. As a result, more heat is being trapped and the earth's temperature is rising. How do we know this? Scientists have been measuring the levels of greenhouse gases in air bubbles in the ice of Antarctica and Greenland over time. They have also studied temperature records and looked at changes in tree rings.

Energy production, factories, and deforestation are major contributors to the production of greenhouse gases.

The effect of humans and animals

Every time we drive a car, use a computer, or cook a meal, we produce greenhouse gases. When factories make all the things we buy and use every day, they pump out polluting gases. When we cut down forests for farming, we release large amounts of carbon into the atmosphere. Although plants counteract the greenhouse effect by converting carbon dioxide into oxygen through photosynthesis, humans are now producing more carbon dioxide than the world's plants can absorb. Methane, another greenhouse gas, traps even more heat than carbon dioxide. It is produced from the garbage we send to landfill sites and by the extraction of coal and natural gas from beneath the ground. Cattle ranching also results in the production of methane,

People living close to nature describe changes in the climate and weather they have never seen before:

"I live in a town called Taloyoak, in northeastern Canada. We hunt and fish. We mainly hunt seals for subsistence. The weather conditions have changed. The wind has changed. The ice breaks up faster. Polar bears are going hungry."

Simon Oleekatalik, Canadian Inuit, 72 years old

"I have been fishing for a living for 16 years. The sea is warming up. Rainfall patterns have really changed in recent years. We have been experiencing more and more storms. Mangroves have been damaged."

Rosenda Aldana, fisherwoman and housewife from Belize, 57 years old

"I have lived here for over 30 years. The temperature of the earth is rising. It is not natural. The glaciers are shrinking rapidly. Kathmandu already has a water shortage problem."

Ngawang Tenzing Jangpo, Abbot of Tengboche monastery, Nepal

especially in the digestive gases emitted by cows. Scientists claim that animals raised for food currently produce between 15 and 20 percent of methane emissions globally.

Severe droughts in countries such as Spain have contributed to an increase in forest fires. A large increase in fires releases more greenhouse gases into the air.

Even if we stop polluting the atmosphere now, the earth's temperature will continue to get warmer because the heat remains trapped in greenhouse gases for decades. But if we act now, the rate of climate change will slow down.

Is warmer weather a bad thing?

Predicting the long-term impact of global warming is a difficult task because the climate is affected by many factors, including seas, ocean currents, prevailing winds, and clouds. Very small changes can have huge effects on what happens in the future. Scientists use computer models to predict possible scenarios. They believe that global average temperatures will rise between 2.5°F and 10.4°F (1.1° C and 5.8° C) over the next hundred years. This does not sound like much, and warmer weather might appear to be an attractive prospect for people living in cool northern countries. But it is extremely significant for the planet and for everyone living on it.

An increase of 3.6° F (2° C) would radically alter our climate. Warmer temperatures are likely to affect ocean currents, which have a big influence on the weather. For example, the Gulf Stream in the Atlantic Ocean brings warm water from the tropics and gives northern countries, such as the United Kingdom, UK, a temperate climate. Some scientists suggest that dramatic changes to the Gulf Stream could leave Europe colder even if the earth heats up. Rising sea levels mean that people living in coastal areas will be affected. Major cities, including New York, London, and Shanghai, could be flooded. Extreme weather events, such as hurricanes and tropical storms, are likely to be more frequent and more intense. By 2080, almost twice as many people worldwide could be exposed to severe flooding from storms.

This satellite image shows Hurricane Floyd cartwheeling toward Florida. With global warming, extreme weather events such as hurricanes, storms, and flooding are on the increase.

Reduction of rainfall in other parts of the world could result in water shortages and drought. Hundreds of millions of people around the world are already facing water shortages, and this problem will increase as temperatures rise. It will also affect the food people grow. Wheat production in India is already declining because of changes in rainfall. Rich countries are the main polluters, but the poorest countries near the equator are hardest hit by droughts and flooding. And the people there cannot afford to adapt their circumstances to these new conditions.

A woman walks along a dried-up riverbed in China. In 2006, sizzling temperatures and the worst drought in 50 years affected southwestern China and many other parts of the world.

FOCUS

A message to the world

Sharon Looremeta is a Maasai woman from Kenya. She works to improve the livelihood of her farming community, which herds cattle as a way of life. There has been a severe drought in Kenya since 2003 and little rain for over three years. Mothers have to take their children out of school to walk for days to find water. Animal carcasses litter the parched land. In July 2007, Live Earth concerts held around the world brought together more than 100 artists and 2 billion people to raise awareness of the impact of global warming. Sharon addressed the world in the UK concert: "My people do not drive 4x4s or pump out excessive emissions, yet mine is one of the communities already being damaged by climate change. Talk will not save my people, only action will."

Global warming threatens the habitats of more than a third of the world's plants and animals and could cause the extinction of many species. Frogs, butterflies, and other animals particularly sensitive to temperatures and droughts will struggle to keep pace with a changing climate. Coral reefs, home to a quarter of all marine life, will be threatened by changes in water temperature and sea levels. In Africa, mosquitoes may take advantage of the changing climate and fly farther afield, carrying diseases such as malaria.

The Belize Barrier Reef is the second largest in the world, after the Great Barrier Reef in Australia. Changes in water temperature and sea levels as a result of global warming could threaten these fragile habitats.

Does everyone agree that the world is warming?

Most scientists and world leaders agree that climate change is occurring and that fossil fuels are to blame. However, despite strong scientific evidence, a small number of influential politicians and business leaders remain unconvinced that the way we produce and use energy is affecting the climate. In their view, the science of global warming is uncertain and the recent increase in the earth's temperature is no cause for alarm. They argue that the earth's atmosphere has experienced many extreme temperature swings between warm periods and ice ages in its 4.5 billion years. So we just need to adapt to a slightly warmer world. It is true that the earth has gone through natural warming and cooling cycles linked to changes in its orbit and the amount of heat received from the sun. But scientific evidence shows that our polluting activities are pushing up temperatures faster than at any time in the last 10,000 years.

Vested interests

A more likely reason for some people to play down the possible effects of global warming is that many countries and individuals have vested interests in the fossil fuel industry. For example, the US government has been reluctant to join international agreements to reduce air pollution. The US economy is based heavily on the oil, coal, and car industries, so it has much to lose if people worldwide reduce their consumption of fossil fuels. When movie star and governor of California Arnold Schwarzenegger called for massive reductions of emissions from cars and trucks, a group of Japanese and US car manufacturers opposed his policies. The doubts aired in the media and in political circles have caused some governments and business leaders to delay taking action to combat climate change. A top British economist, Nicholas Stern, managed to convince some of the doubters by demonstrating that the costs of global warming are doubling every decade and could reach hundreds of billions of dollars each year if people do not take action.

FORUM

People have very different opinions about the level of threat posed by climate change:

"Climate change is the most severe problem we are facing today—more serious even than the threat of terrorism."

David King, chief scientific adviser to the UK government, 2004

"It would be a terrible mistake to rush into the development of energy alternatives when the consequences of global warming are still not fully understood."

Rex W. Tillerson, chief executive of Exxon Mobil, 2007

What's your opinion?

In July 2005, Thunder Horse, the world's largest semi-submersible oil platform, was hit by Hurricane Dennis in the Gulf of Mexico.

Chapter 4

How can we turn down the heat?

Global warming is a global problem. It makes no difference whether the pollution comes from Chinese factories or North American cars; all humans need to take action to reduce their impact on an overheating world.

What is the Kyoto Protocol?

In 1997, more than 160 industrialized countries met in Kyoto, Japan, to discuss the problem of climate change. They agreed to cut back their emissions of greenhouse gases by about 5 percent (compared to those in the year 1990). The international agreement was formally adopted and called the Kyoto Protocol. Some experts claim that the reductions called for at Kyoto are not drastic enough. Even so, some industrialized countries have not joined the agreement. These countries include the United States, one of the biggest polluters in the world. China, India, and other developing countries were not included in the protocol because, historically, they have not made a serious contribution to greenhouse gas emissions.

A principle of the Kyoto Protocol is that industrialized countries must help poorer countries gain access to clean energy. It suggests that industrialized countries can trade "carbon credits" instead of reducing their own emissions. For example, a coal power station in the UK could offset (balance

FOCUS

A brickyard with a difference

Sanjay Sharma owns a brickyard in Kaithun in northeast India. With the help of the Kyoto Protocol, Sanjay is expanding his business by buying new kilns that use less coal and do not pollute the atmosphere. In return for the 550 tons (500 metric tons) of carbon he is saving, Sanjay will receive ten years of funding from a Canadian company. "Soon, the road to the brickyard will be bordered by small brick houses," says Sanjay. It would take 17 Indian people to produce the same level of emissions as one Canadian person, so Sanjay believes the business deal he has made is fair.

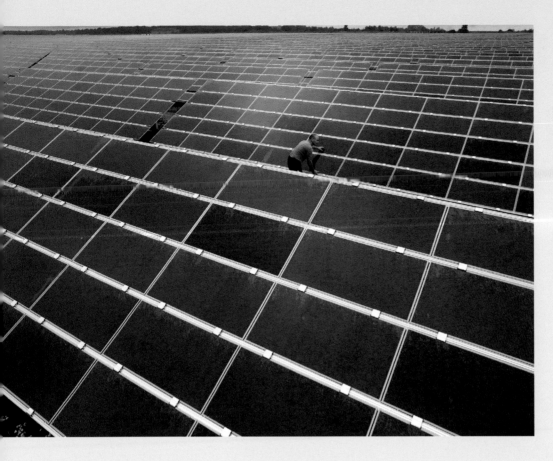

Many countries are choosing to opt for solar energy. The Waldpolenz Solar Park in Germany (to be completed in 2009) will be the world's largest solar power plant. It is roughly the size of 200 football fields placed side by side.

the effect of) its pollution by investing in cleaner technology abroad; for example by funding a solar power plant in China. The protocol states that countries must meet their targets by 2012. It is an important first step toward worldwide cooperation concerning emissions control. International talks for another treaty with additional targets got under way in Bali in December 2007. Meanwhile, governments around the world are taking different actions to reduce energy use and find alternatives to fossil fuels.

Staying cool

Many governments believe the priority is to keep polluting gases from reaching the atmosphere. Therefore, energy companies are investigating ways to capture emissions from power stations and bury them in the ground or at the bottom of the ocean. Projects are being pioneered in the North Sea and the United States. Environmentalists warn that this will require a lot of energy and that there is the danger of long-term leaks into the atmosphere. The car industry is looking at new ways to power vehicles more efficiently. Eco-friendly cars that run on cleaner fuels are appearing on the roads. It is now possible to buy an electric car powered by rechargeable batteries or a hybrid car powered by both electricity and gas.

Other types of car, popular in South America and India, are powered by compressing methane extracted from natural gas, which produces fewer emissions than gas. This is the main source of fuel for all buses in India's capital city, New Delhi. There are also cars that run on biofuel made from plants such as corn, sugarcane and rapeseed oil. In theory, the carbon dioxide emitted by such a car is equivalent to the carbon dioxide absorbed by the plants grown for fuel. It means that this type of car is carbon neutral.

At a fuel station in Jameln, Germany, a car is filled with biogas made from slurry (waste digested by bacteria), ryegrass, and corn. This was the first filling station to sell biogas from renewable resources.

The problems with biofuel

In countries such as the United States and Brazil, which rely heavily on gasoline, the production of biofuel is increasing. In 2006, more than one-third of the entire US corn crop was used to produce biofuel. But problems remain concerning how and where the crops are grown. To grow crops, farmers need diesel to fuel their tractors, then the fuel companies need fossil fuels to power their distilleries and more diesel to transport the fuel to its destination. The production of biofuel could use more energy than it produces! The process could also be catastrophic if we started growing crops for fuel rather than for food or if we cleared forests to grow more crops. In Indonesia and Malaysia, large areas of the rain forest have been cleared to grow palm oil for the production of biofuel. Cutting down forests destroys habitats, and the burning of stubble pollutes the environment.

Green thinking

Aviation is the fastest-growing form of transportation. About 3.5 percent of greenhouse gases comes from aircraft, so the industry is trying to find ways to cut down on fuel consumption and reduce emissions. Engineers are experimenting with new shapes of planes, lighter materials, more efficient engines, and different types of fuel.

Scientists have been exploring even more radical ways of removing carbon from the atmosphere. They are looking at ways of using giant mirrors orbiting in space to prevent the sun's heat from reaching the earth. Some environmentalists have suggested submerging millions of large plastic tubes in the world's oceans. These would bring nutrients from deep water to the surface, which would encourage algae to bloom and absorb carbon dioxide. A top scientist is researching how we can create artificial organisms that could gobble up carbon dioxide or even create electricity.

Expert View

Some scientists believe that the nuclear option is the key to providing sufficient clean energy for the future:

"Large-scale nuclear power is the only practical way that we have to solve the greenhouse gas problem."

James Lovelock, scientist and environmentalist, 2000

The nuclear option—a heated debate

Many people, including some environmentalists, believe we need to give nuclear power another chance to prove its worth. There are about 400 nuclear power plants in the world today, providing up to 6 percent of the world's energy. By building more nuclear plants, we could bridge the gap between fossil fuels and the large-scale use of renewable energy. Nuclear power produces massive amounts of power with hardly any carbon emissions. In 1990, France shut down its last coal mine and now obtains 80 percent of its electricity from nuclear power.

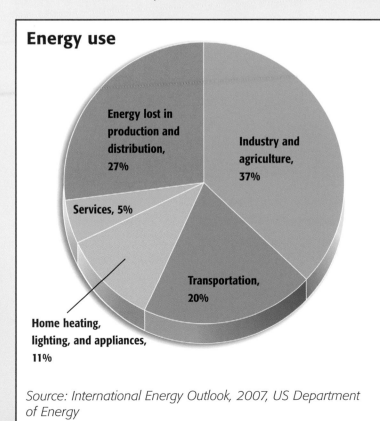

Energy use

Energy lost in production and distribution, 27%

Industry and agriculture, 37%

Services, 5%

Transportation, 20%

Home heating, lighting, and appliances, 11%

Source: International Energy Outlook, 2007, US Department of Energy

This pie chart shows the amount of energy used for different activities. About a third of our energy is used to produce goods and grow food. About one-quarter of the energy is lost during production and distribution.

By 2050, India plans to obtain 25 percent of its electricity from nuclear power. There is a heated debate about the use of nuclear power because of the problem of storing dangerous waste, the potential for accidents, and the possibility that it could lead to an increase in the manufacture and use of nuclear weapons. For example, countries such as Iran are discouraged from developing nuclear power because other nations fear they might want to build nuclear weapons.

Star power

Nuclear fusion is a new form of nuclear power. It is the same power that fuels the sun and the stars. If two atoms are joined (rather than split), huge amounts of energy can be released. One pound (half a kilogram) of fusion fuel would produce the same amount of energy as 22,100,000 pounds (10,000,000 kilograms) of fossil fuel. To produce this type of energy, hydrogen atoms need to be heated up to 180 million degrees Farenheit (100 million degrees Celsius). The United States, Russia, Europe, Japan, China, and other countries are making plans for the first fusion reactor to be in France. The advantage is that fusion fuel produces less radioactive waste, but the technology is very expensive and still in development.

In 2006, Chinese scientists working with researchers from other countries built an experimental fusion reactor in Anhui, eastern China. This is a smaller version of the reactor that will be built in France.

Saving the rain forests

Like the oceans, the world's forests regulate earth's climate. They store massive amounts of carbon, and this helps to cool the planet. Each year, large areas of rain forest are being cleared for cattle ranching, farming, and logging. When a forest is burned to make room for a soybean field or a cattle pasture, the carbon rises into the atmosphere as carbon dioxide. The loss of rain forests around the world accounts for about one-fifth of all emissions; that is more than the transportation sector. Yet this type of pollution

The Amazon rain forest, the largest tropical rain forest in the world, is being destroyed at the equivalent of 3,600 football fields a day.

receives little attention in the news compared with the pollution from transportation. Stopping the destruction of the rain forest is one of the most effective ways to reduce global carbon emissions. If the forest disappears it will not only be a disaster for the millions of people living there but will also have a catastrophic effect on the stability of the world's climate.

Governments of developing countries such as Guyana, with large areas of rain forest, claim they are being asked to protect their forests for the benefit of the whole world. However, they argue that they have made a very small contribution to global greenhouse gas emissions. Eight tropical countries, with 80 percent of the world's remaining tropical forest, have formed an alliance to make sure that forest conservation is included in international talks on climate change. They are asking for financial help and clean technologies from industrialized nations and in return say they will protect their forests.

Expert View

Protecting the rain forest is essential for the earth's future:

"If we lose the world's rain forests, we lose the fight against climate change. Rain forests are our earth's greatest utility—our planet's lungs, thermostat, and air conditioning system."

Michael Somare, prime minister of Papua New Guinea, September 2007

Energy all around us

In many countries, renewable energy has already provided a solution for the future. Wind power is a fast-growing sector, and modern wind turbines now generate electricity for thousands of homes. For example, wind power produces 20 percent of all Denmark's electricity. But some people argue that wind farms are ugly and noisy and occupy a lot of land. About 17 acres of land are needed for an average wind farm, which can provide electricity for up to 1,000 homes. If there is no wind or if the wind is unreliably gusty, another source of energy is needed to supplement the wind power. For this reason, offshore wind farms are becoming more popular.

FORUM

Some people think we can combat global warming by using new forms of energy; others think we should all just use less:

"Keeping America competitive requires affordable energy. America is addicted to oil, which is often imported from unstable parts of the world. The best way to break this addiction is through technology."

President George W. Bush, 2006

"These technological developments are no substitute for reducing our emissions and changing our energy-producing and -consuming culture substantially."

Doug Parr, scientist, Greenpeace, 2007

What do you think?

Another increasingly important energy source is solar power. Solar panels convert sunlight into electricity and can be used to provide heat and hot water for homes. The Japanese government plans to install solar panels on the roofs of a million homes. Large solar power plants have been built in areas with a high level of sunshine, such as the Californian desert. But on cloudy days and during the night, other sources of power are needed to create energy. Storing and transporting solar energy is very expensive and inefficient.

Energy from earth and sea

In countries with volcanic landscapes, such as Iceland and New Zealand, geothermal energy is an important power source, using the earth's internal heat to create electricity and heat buildings. In Iceland, 90 percent of the buildings are heated by geothermal energy. It is also possible to produce electricity by harnessing energy from tides and waves. Tidal power stations are already operating in Canada, France, Russia, and China, but the technology is very expensive.

Swirling water enters through the sluice gates of a tidal barrage on the Rance River in France. Turbines use the energy of the tides going in and out to generate electricity.

Biomass

Finally, the use of biomass to produce electricity is increasing in many countries. Wood and straw are burned in power stations to create electricity and heat. Manure, farming, and food waste are converted into biofuels. In 2006, a company in San Francisco, launched a program with the idea of using the methane produced from dog waste to heat homes and produce electricity. The solution for the future might be a combination of different renewable sources of energy. They are clean, safe, and will never run out, and the technology needed to produce them already exists. Renewables are still very expensive, but the more we use this kind of energy, the cheaper it will become. Governments need to take the lead in investing in these technologies and making them more available so that people are encouraged to use them.

Chapter 5

What about the future?

Imagine yourself in decades to come. You leave home in your new eco-friendly car, then run out of fuel. But instead of having to walk miles to a garage, you can stop at a friend's house and borrow a hydrogen generator to refuel your car. Hydrogen, the most abundant element on earth, may become an important fuel for car and aircraft transportation in years to come. It could also provide heat and electricity for our homes.

The new wonder fuel?

Hydrogen can be found in various resources, such as water, natural gas, and plants, so every country has a source of hydrogen. The sun is a giant ball of mainly hydrogen gases, a vivid example of the huge amount of potential energy there is in this element. Like fossil fuels, hydrogen can be burned directly or converted into electricity through batteries or fuel cells. The problem is that unlike fossil fuels, it cannot be drilled or pumped out of the ground. It can only be found in combination with other elements and so needs to be extracted using a different source of energy. If this energy source is renewable, then hydrogen could become a clean fuel for the future—the only waste would be water!

This BMW sports car, with its aerodynamic design and light aluminum body, is powered entirely by the clean process of liquid-hydrogen combustion. It has already set nine speed records of 186 miles per hour (300 km per hour) and above.

About 90 percent of homes in Iceland are heated by geothermal power. By 2050, Iceland wants to become the first country in the world to stop using fossil fuels completely.

Today hydrogen produced from natural gas is used as a fuel by industry in metal refining and food processing. The US space program also uses hydrogen fuel cells to power space shuttles into orbit. The fuel cells provide heat and electricity for the shuttle, and astronauts use the pure water exhaust from the fuel cells as drinking water. Portable fuel cells are used to provide longer-lasting power for laptop computers and cell phones and on military maneuvers. Small fuel cells have the potential to power electric cars. Large fuel cells can provide electricity in remote places where there are no power lines.

In the United States, hydrogen-powered buses and cars are starting to appear on the roads. The United States has launched a billion-dollar program to develop hydrogen-fueled vehicles. Car manufacturers have already designed a hydrogen generator no bigger than a refrigerator that works with electricity. Hydrogen is reliable and safe to manufacture and has a minimum impact on the environment. But the technology is expensive, and it will take a few decades for hydrogen-powered cars to become affordable or energy to be widely available from hydrogen power plants. Argentina is leading the way in this field by using its abundant supply of geothermal energy to produce hydrogen. But this clean form of energy will only become popular if renewable energy is affordable and widespread elsewhere in the world.

Expert View

A hydrogen-powered future seems the obvious solution to many business leaders:

'We are at the peak of the oil age but the beginning of the hydrogen age. The transition will be very messy, and will take many technological paths but the future will be hydrogen cells.'

Herman Kuuipers, Manager of Exploratory Research for Royal Dutch Shell, a multinational oil company, 2001

From global to local

The secret of energy's future may be locked in the past: in other words, in a return to generating energy within a short distance of where people live. We could try to meet some of our energy needs by installing solar panels and miniature wind turbines on the roofs of our houses and drawing up the earth's heat with an underground pump. Energy on our doorstep means that less heat is wasted in the production and distribution system. Communities could be responsible for producing power with, for example, their own wind farms, hydrogen supply networks, and fuel cells. In Denmark, the Netherlands, and Sweden, a number of towns and cities have embarked on the local generation of energy. They use hundreds of smaller scale heat and power plants near homes and offices, and because the wind does not always blow and the sun does not always shine, they are also connected to national electricity grids as a backup.

FORUM

Some experts think our future energy needs can be answered by nuclear power. Others say we need to take local and personal responsibility for our energy requirements:

"Renewable sources, including sun, wind, and biomass, would all require vast amounts of land if developed up to large-scale production—unlike nuclear power."

Jesse Ausubel, American conservation biologist and climate change researcher, 2007

"Rather than waiting for government and vested interests to deliver too little, too late, decentralized energy means communities, towns, and cities can take action today."

Stephen Tindale, director, UK Greenpeace, 2006

What do you think?

Grand designs

Technology alone will not solve the problem of our future energy needs. Most of us live in cities that are becoming taller, bigger, and more densely populated. We therefore need to rethink the way we design and plan our homes and communities so that we can reduce our energy use and tap into different forms of energy. We can construct our homes, schools, and offices to make best use of the power and light of the sun. We can ensure that new buildings and alterations to existing ones are energy efficient. Eventually the buildings in which we live, work, or go to school could become small power stations generating their own energy supply. The most sustainable skyscraper to date, the Pearl River Tower, is being built in Guangzhou, China. The facade is designed to funnel wind, which powers turbines that generate energy for the building's heating, ventilation, and air-

The rooftop solar panels on these houses in a town in Switzerland use sunlight to heat water supplies for each home. This saves energy, reduces heating costs, and avoids the use of energy power that produces pollution.

conditioning systems. It is also designed to channel power from the sun. The tower will use at least 60 percent less energy than a normal building. Another building, in the UK, uses an idea from nature in its design. The architects who designed Portcullis House in London, imitated the ventilation system used by termites in their mounds.

In addition to environmentally friendly buildings, we can plan our communities so that we do not need to commute long distances to school or work. We also need to rethink our public transportation systems. In the Netherlands, Germany, Switzerland, and Denmark, buses are scheduled to meet trains; bicycles can be transported free of charge on trains, streetcars and buses; and continuous bicycle lanes stretch across entire cities. More than 70 towns in France are returning to one of the oldest and greenest forms of transportation, the humble horse, and people are using these animals to pull school buses and trash carts.

Chapter 6

What can you do to help?

Every time we use energy, we release greenhouse gases into the atmosphere. We can calculate the amount we produce by using a carbon footprint, which measures the impact our activities have on the environment in units of carbon dioxide and other greenhouse gases. By reducing our carbon footprint, we can save energy and help to combat climate change.

How big is your footprint?

You can measure your emissions when you travel by car, throw trash in the bin or buy strawberries that have been grown abroad. For example, one year's driving produces 11,000 pounds (5,000 kg) of carbon, and every bag of garbage produces 44 pounds (20 kg) of carbon. A person's carbon

By limiting our own energy use, we can reduce our carbon footprint and to combat climate change. For every journey under 3 miles (5 km) that we walk instead of drive, we save about 4 pounds (2 kg) of carbon.

FOCUS

A carbon-neutral house in London

Donnachadh McCarthy has turned his 165-year-old London home into a carbon-neutral house. He has installed a system to harvest rainwater for domestic use, a wind turbine, a solar system for electricity and heat, and a wood burner. He has also insulated his walls and loft and double-glazed his windows. He gets the logs for his fire from local waste timber. He does not own a car; instead he has his organic fruit and vegetables delivered by bicycle. Last year, Donnachadh produced only half a can of unrecycled trash.

footprint varies depending on where and how he or she lives. The average footprint in Western Europe is about 13 tons (12 metric tons), or 26,500 pounds (12,000 kg), of carbon per year. This is the same as 240,000 balloons of greenhouse gases. The average American or Australian person produces twice as much, mainly because they drive farther and use bigger cars. If you want to calculate your carbon footprint, use a search engine on the Internet to find a reliable carbon calculator. You can compare your carbon footprint with the carbon footprint of your friends and other people around the world.

Save energy at home

Once you know the size and impact of your footprint, your own actions, combined with those of others, can bring about huge changes. About a fifth of our emissions come from heating, lighting, and powering our homes. So we can start by trying to use less energy at home. Each household in the UK creates about 5.0 tons (4.5 metric tons) of carbon a year just for heating. By turning down thermostats and making sure our homes are well insulated, we can help reduce this. The four biggest energy guzzlers in most houses are refrigerators, clothes dryers, computers, and lighting. Switch off lights, and tell the rest of your family to do the same.

These pie charts show the amount of greenhouse gas emissions produced by the average person in the US and the UK. Different countries use different amounts of energy and have a different impact on the global environment.

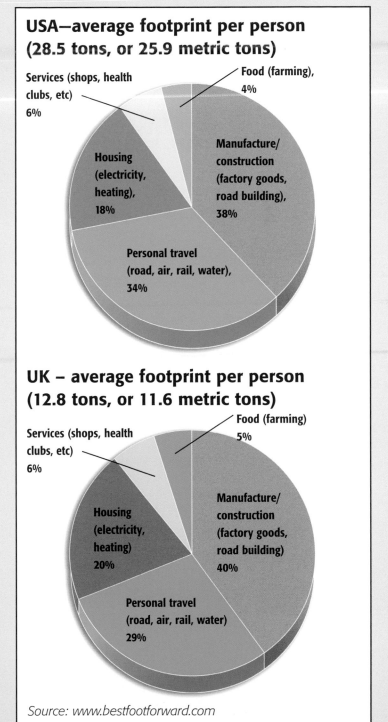

USA—average footprint per person (28.5 tons, or 25.9 metric tons)

Services (shops, health clubs, etc) 6%

Food (farming), 4%

Housing (electricity, heating), 18%

Manufacture/ construction (factory goods, road building), 38%

Personal travel (road, air, rail, water), 34%

UK – average footprint per person (12.8 tons, or 11.6 metric tons)

Services (shops, health clubs, etc) 6%

Food (farming) 5%

Housing (electricity, heating) 20%

Manufacture/ construction (factory goods, road building) 40%

Personal travel (road, air, rail, water) 29%

Source: www.bestfootforward.com

Researchers study a range of energy-efficient lightbulbs. One of the best actions we can take to save energy and reduce our electricity bills is to replace all our lightbulbs with energy-efficient models.

Change to energy-efficient lightbulbs: they may cost more, but they last longer and use a fraction of the energy of ordinary lightbulbs. Many countries, including Japan, Venezuela, Cuba, Australia, and Ireland, have banned the use of inefficient lightbulbs. Switch off your computer completely when you are not using it. Even if you do not have solar panels on your roof yet, you can still use the sun as a source of energy. Start by hanging out your wash on a clothesline rather than tumble drying it. Use a solar calculator and a solar power charger for your MP3 player, laptop, and cell phone. The same energy tips can be used on the appliances in your school.

Greener ways to get around

Transportation accounts for nearly a third of our emissions and is the fastest-growing source of greenhouse gases. So it is a good idea to reduce your number of car trips. If you can, walk, bicycle, run, roller-skate, or use public transportation. If you need to drive, share a car with friends. If your family is thinking of buying a new car, suggest getting an eco-friendly vehicle that runs on "clean" fuel. Better still, consider whether you really need to buy a new car, since between 3.3 and 5.5 tons (3.0 and 5.0 metric tons) of carbon dioxide are produced each time one is manufactured. An obvious way to reduce your carbon footprint is to travel by plane less frequently. Air travel produces three times more carbon dioxide per person and per half mile (kilometer) than train travel. Planes also pipe greenhouse gases into the earth's upper atmosphere, which is where they do the most damage. One flight from New York to London can

The pie chart on the right shows the energy used in our homes. More than 75 per cent is used on heating, cooling and lighting. We need to try to use and lose less energy.

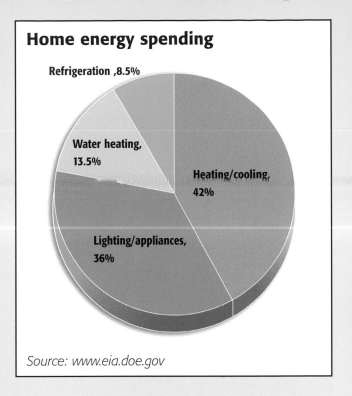

Home energy spending

Refrigeration ,8.5%

Water heating, 13.5%

Heating/cooling, 42%

Lighting/appliances, 36%

Source: www.eia.doe.gov

represent the same or an even larger footprint as driving a car for a whole year.

Consumer responsibilities

Simple decisions, such as what we eat and what we buy, can have an impact on our carbon footprint. We buy clothes made in China, bottles of water from volcanic springs, and green beans grown in Mexico. It takes huge amounts of energy to make and distribute all these items. If we think about where things come from and how they are made, we can begin to understand the links between the use of energy, the production of waste, and the wider issue of climate change. As consumers, we can make a difference by choosing products with the smallest carbon footprints. Something as simple as carrying a bottle of water with you, so that you do not have to rely on store-bought water, can help reduce your own carbon footprint.

FOCUS

The carbon footprint of potato chips

To help us make the right choices, a number of companies are investigating ways to indicate the carbon footprint of their products. Coca-Cola, Cadbury's Dairy Milk chocolate, and Andrex toilet paper could soon carry labels revealing their carbon footprint. Walkers, a British company, is the first big company to use labeling; in their case, it states the carbon emissions released in the production of their potato chips. One bag of cheese and onion potato chips has a carbon footprint of 2.6 ounces (75 g), measured from the point at which the potato and sunflower seeds are sown through transportation, to final disposal of the bag.

Shop locally

As a general rule, the food that has traveled the shortest distance to reach you is the best for your health and for the climate. Therefore, one way to reduce your carbon footprint is to buy food produced locally and in season. But you also need to know how the food is produced. If it is grown with fertilizers or in a heated greenhouse, it might be healthier and better for the environment to choose imported foods that have not been produced in this way. So, if you live in Sweden, it is better to buy tomatoes grown in Spain than tomatoes grown in a Swedish greenhouse. And maybe we should think about changing our eating habits. Do we really need to eat tomatoes in the winter or any fruit out of its natural season?

If there is a farmer's market near where you live or a local home delivery system, try it out. You could even take more radical action and reduce your footprint by eating more

The eco-village of Ithaca, in New York, is part of a global movement of communities that have decided to reduce their impact on the environment. The village has an organic farm for local residents and is designed to encourage community life. Residents each volunteer a few hours per week to work in the village.

local fruit and vegetables and less meat. Meat production is extremely energy intensive. A beefburger, for example, produces up to 7 pounds (3 kg) of carbon. This is generated by the growing of crops for cattle feed and the use of energy in the slaughtering, freezing, transporting, and storing processes—not to mention the energy used in the cooking process and in the production of wheat for the burger bun. Add to this the methane naturally emitted by cattle, and you end up with an incredible 60 carbon balloons every time you eat a burger!

Small, green, and local

Instead of producing a large amount of power in a few places, we need to produce a little green, local power everywhere. An increasing number of communities are adopting these principles across the world. Why not try spreading these ideas in your local area? There is no single solution to the problem of dwindling energy resources and the impact of emissions on global warming. There are, however, many different views on the matter, and oil companies, politicians, and environmentalists, to name but a few, will all want to make their voices heard. We can help in the energy crisis by looking at the facts, forming our own opinions, and making sure we take action at home, at school, and in our communities. Encourage others to do the same, including your teachers, local retailers, and politicians. Talk about energy with your family, friends, and neighbors. Find out about the energy policy in your school and join an environmental campaign group, encouraging governments to act. Before long, saving energy will be second nature to us all and part of our everyday lives. It is clear that we will eventually run out of fossil fuels, but as long as the sun shines, we will not run out of energy. We simply need to be imaginative about how we produce and use new sources of energy in the future.

FORUM

Some experts believe that individuals will readily take action to safeguard the earth's future and conserve energy. Others think government action is essential if people are to change their ways:

"Each one of us is a cause of global warming. So each one of us can make choices to change that. The solutions are in our hands. We just need to have determination to make it happen."

Al Gore, former US vice-president, 2006

"Manmade global warming cannot be restrained unless we persuade the government to force us to change the way we live."

George Monbiot, British journalist, 2007

What do you think?

Glossary

alternative fuel A fuel made from natural gas or biomass.

atomic bomb A nuclear weapon in which enormous energy is released by nuclear fission.

biofuel A fuel made from plants or household and animal waste. Examples of biofuel include bio-ethanol, made from sugarcane, wheat, or corn, and bio-diesel, made from vegetable oils such as rapeseed or palm oil or waste cooking oils.

biomass Anything derived from plant or animal matter; waste from agricultural crops, wood, and animals.

carbon capture The removal of carbon dioxide from fossil fuels, either before or after they are burned.

carbon dioxide A colorless gas produced by all living creatures and emitted when fossil fuels such coal, gas, and oil are burned.

carbon footprint A way to measure the amount of carbon dioxide produced as a result of human activities.

climate change Change to the earth's climate, mainly as a result of the emission of greenhouse gases.

coal A fossil fuel formed from the remains of trees and ferns trapped underground and compressed by heat and pressure.

coal-fired power plant A power plant that uses coal as fuel to generate electricity.

deforestation The removal of trees from forested land.

developed countries The wealthiest nations in the world, including Western Europe, the US, Canada, Japan, Australia, and New Zealand.

developing countries Less economically developed countries, including India, China and many African countries.

energy efficiency The saving of energy through activities such as the use of high-efficiency appliances, energy-saving lightbulbs, and efficient building design.

fossil fuels Fuels such as oil, coal and natural gas, formed from the fossilized remains of plants and animals.

fuel cell A battery that produces electricity from hydrogen and air, with water as the only waste.

geothermal energy Energy produced by natural processes inside the earth. Geothermal energy can be taken from hot springs, reservoirs of hot water deep below the ground, or by breaking open the rock itself.

global warming An increase in the temperature of the earth. Global warming has occurred in the distant past as s result of the earth's natural cycles, but today the term is used to refer to the warming linked to human activity.

greenhouse effect The effect of gases in the earth's atmosphere that trap heat from the sun.

greenhouse gases Gases that trap the sun's heat in the atmosphere.

hybrid car A vehicle that uses batteries or fuel cells as part of its power source, combined with gas or diesel.

hydrogen The lightest gas and most abundant element in the universe, found in different resources, including water, natural gas, and plants.

hydropower Energy harnessed from moving water and used to generate electricity.

Industrial Revolution The rapid development of industry during the early nineteenth century, which took place as a result of the introduction of machines into factories.

insulation Materials used in buildings to conserve heat.

kerosene A thick oil obtained from crude oil and used as a fuel.

krill Small shrimplike creatures that live near the surface of the earth's oceans.

Kyoto Protocol An international agreement to cut overall greenhouse gas emissions, signed by many of the world's countries in 1997.

natural gas A fossil fuel formed from the remains of tiny marine animals buried at the bottom of the ocean and compressed by heat and pressure.

nonrenewable Something that cannot be replaced.

nuclear fission Energy that comes from splitting atoms of radioactive materials, such as uranium.

nuclear fusion Combining atoms to release large amounts of energy. The technology is still in an experimental stage.

oil A black, liquid fossil fuel found deep in the earth. Gasoline and most plastics are made from oil.

photosynthesis The process by which plants convert sunlight, water, and carbon dioxide into food, oxygen, and water. They "breathe in" carbon dioxide and "breathe out" oxygen.

power plant A facility where power, especially electricity, is generated.

radioactivity The high-speed transmission of energy in the form of particles or electromagnetic waves.

renewable energy Energy taken from a resource that is naturally replenished and will not run out.

solar energy Energy from the sun that can be converted into heat or electricity.

turbine A device with blades that is turned by wind, water, or high-pressure steam.

United Nations An international organization established in 1945 to work toward maintaining international peace and security and economic and social cooperation.

Further information

Books

David, Laurie, and Cambria Gordon. *The Down-to-Earth Guide to Global Warming.* Scholastic, 2007.

I Count. *I Count—Your Step-by-Step Guide to Climate Bliss.* Penguin, 2006

Films

An Inconvenient Truth. Laurence Bender Productions, 2006
   Directed by David Guggenheim, this documentary concerns the efforts of former US vice president Al Gore to expose the myths about global warming and inspire people to take action.

Websites

www.energyquest.ca.gov
   An energy education website produced by the California Energy Commission.

www.nef.org.uk
   A website produced by the National Energy Foundation, including a section for schools, with information about climate change and how to cut carbon emissions.

www.climatecrisis.net
   A website to accompany the film *An Inconvenient Truth*, providing useful information about the science of global warming and tips on how to take action.

www.eere.energy.gov/kids/
   US Department of Energy website, with games, tips, and facts for children who want to save energy.

www.managenergy.net/kidscorner
   European Commission website, with information, games, and photos about energy.

www.eia.doe.gov/kids/energyfacts
   US government Energy Information Administration website, providing useful facts and information about energy.

www.myfootprint.org
   A site to help you calculate your carbon footprint.

www.edenproject.com
   A website produced by the Eden Project, UK, with information on energy and climate change.

www.globalcool.org/
   Tips on how to use and lose less energy by doing any or many of several easy things.

www.sciencemuseum.org.uk
   Science Museum website, with information about energy, from the first steam engines to ways of fuelling the future.

Index